2/11/13

MARY McLEOD BETHUNE

WOMAN OF COURAGE

Louisburg Library
Bringing People and Information Together

Famous
African Americans

**Patricia and
Fredrick McKissack**

Enslow Elementary
an imprint of

Enslow Publishers, Inc.
40 Industrial Road
Box 398
Berkeley Heights, NJ 07922
USA

http://www.enslow.com

To our friends Linda and Rob

Enslow Elementary, an imprint of Enslow Publishers, Inc.

Enslow Elementary® is a registered trademark of Enslow Publishers, Inc.

Original edition published as *Mary McLeod Bethune: A Great Teacher* in 1991.

Library of Congress Cataloging-in-Publication Data

McKissack, Pat, 1944–
    Mary McLeod Bethune : woman of courage / Patricia and Frederick McKissack.
        pages cm. — (Famous African Americans)
    Includes index.
    Summary: "Read about Mary McLeod Bethune's life. Discover how she started a school, and worked in the White House"—Provided by publisher.
    ISBN 978-0-7660-4103-5
    1. Bethune, Mary McLeod, 1875–1955—Juvenile literature. 2. African American women educators—Biography—Juvenile literature. 3. African American women social reformers—Biography—Juvenile literature. 4. Teachers—United States—Biography—Juvenile literature. I. McKissack, Fredrick. II. Title.
    E185.97.B34M38 2013
    370.92—dc23
        [B]
                        2012007620

Future editions:
Paperback ISBN 978-1-4644-0204-3
ePUB ISBN 978-1-4645-1117-2
PDF ISBN 978-1-4646-1117-9

Printed in the United States of America

082012 Lake Book Manufacturing, Inc., Melrose Park, IL

10 9 8 7 6 5 4 3 2 1

♻ Enslow Publishers, Inc., is committed to printing our books on recycled paper. The paper in every book contains 10% to 30% post-consumer waste (PCW). The cover board on the outside of each book contains 100% PCW. Our goal is to do our part to help young people and the environment too!

Photo Credits: Library of Congress, Prints and Photographs, p. 20; Moorland-Spingarn Research Center, Howard University, p. 16; State Archives of Florida, pp. 1, 3, 4, 10, 14.

Illustration Credits: Ned O., pp. 7, 8, 13, 18

Cover Photo: State Archives of Florida

Series Consultant:
Russell Adams, PhD
Emeritus Professor
Afro-American Studies
Howard University

CONTENTS

Mary Jane McLeod grew up in this log cabin in Mayesville, South Carolina.

I WILL READ!

· ·

It was the summer of 1875. Patsy and Sam McLeod's (sounds like Mac-Loud) fifteenth child was born. Her name was Mary Jane McLeod.

It was a happy time for the family. Patsy and Sam had been **slaves**. Mary Jane was their first child born free! That made Mary Jane McLeod special.

Mary Jane grew up in a large and loving family in Mayesville, South Carolina. She rode Old Bush, the family mule, to the fields. She picked cotton along with her brothers and sisters on her father's farm.

One day Mary Jane went with her mother to a large house. Her mother washed and ironed for the people who lived there. Mary Jane had never been in such a big house. A young girl who lived there showed Mary Jane around.

There was a book on a table. Mary Jane opened it. Suddenly the girl took it away, saying, "Put that book down! You can't read it anyway!"

Mary Jane was surprised and hurt. True, she couldn't read. But why did picking up the book make the other girl so angry?

The McLeods had a Bible. Nobody could read it. That night, Mary Jane held the book in her hand. "I will read!" she said. "God willing, I will read!"

As a young girl, Mary Jane decided that she would learn how to read.

CHAPTER 2
SCHOOL DAYS

One day Miss Emma Wilson came to Mayesville. She told Sam and Patsy about the school she was starting. Would they send Mary Jane to school?

Sam didn't think so. He needed everybody to help in the fields. Mary Jane prayed softly. Patsy spoke to Sam alone. At last Sam gave in. Mary Jane could go to school.

Mary Jane's brothers and sisters were disappointed. Why couldn't she read after the first day in school? It took time. Before long Mary Jane did learn how to read and write. On one special night, she read the Bible to her mother and father. They were so proud.

Miss Wilson's school went to the sixth grade. A kind woman paid for Mary Jane to go to the **Scotia Seminary** in Concord, North Carolina. So in 1887 Mary Jane went away to school.

As a young woman, Mary Jane wanted to teach and help others.

She was just twelve years old. It was so lonely at first. She missed her family very much. Seven years later Mary finished Scotia. Then she went to **Moody Bible College** in Chicago. Mary Jane McLeod was ready to start her life's work. But what would it be? she wondered.

CHAPTER 3
A DREAM AND $1.50

Mary wanted to teach in Africa. Instead she took a teaching job in Georgia. Good teachers were needed there.

Mary met Albertus Bethune. He was a teacher too. He made her laugh. They were happy together. In 1898 Mary and Albertus married. A year later, their son was born. His name was Albert McLeod Bethune. Everyone called him Bert.

Mrs. Bethune had heard that there was no school for black children in Daytona Beach, Florida. Mrs. Bethune went there.

"I want to start a school for Negro girls," she said. All she had was $1.50. Some people laughed. Others helped.

Mrs. Bethune would not give up her dream. First she rented a small house. She found writing paper in the trash.

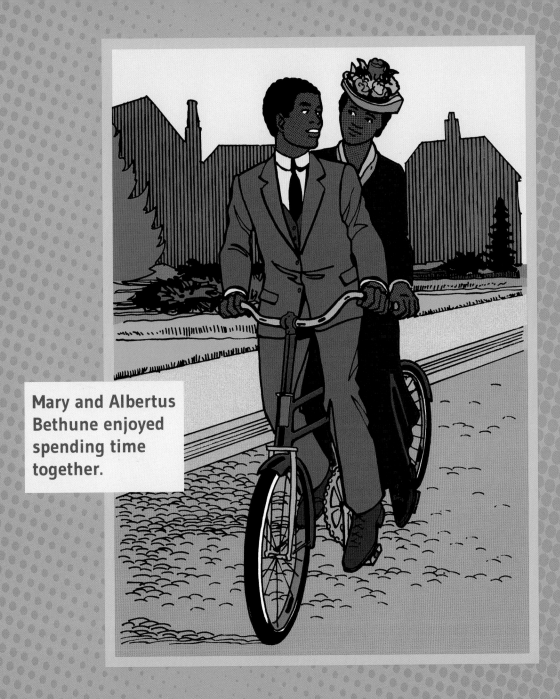

Mary and Albertus Bethune enjoyed spending time together.

Mrs. Bethune worked hard to start a school for black girls. Here she stands with her students.

She had to use boxes for desks and coal for pencils. It was a poor beginning.

But on October 3, 1904, Mrs. Bethune opened her school. She had five students. By 1905 the school had one hundred students and three teachers.

Next she bought land that had been the city trash dump. That is where she would build her school. Some people laughed. But others helped. Rich, important people gave money to help build her school . . . and a hospital, too.

The first building for the school was finished in 1906. It was called Faith Hall, because faith had built it.

Mrs. Bethune was a good speaker. She spoke at churches and schools all over the country.

CHAPTER 4

THE BLACK ROSE

In 1923, Mrs. Bethune's school joined with Cookman, an all-boys school. Bethune-Cookman became a grade school, high school, and college. Boys and girls went to school together.

Mrs. Bethune was the school's first president. But to her students, she was always just "Mother Dear."

Another name for Mrs. Bethune was "The Black Rose." This is how she got that name.

Mrs. Bethune spoke all over the country. One idea she talked about was a big "people garden." She said that people are like flowers. They live together in the world just as flowers grow in a garden. Red, yellow, small, tall—all growing together. They are all different. But each one is lovely.

Mrs. Bethune dreamed of a "people garden" where everyone could live together in peace.

Once a child said to Mrs. Bethune that blacks couldn't live in the "people garden." There were no black flowers! This made Mrs. Bethune feel sad. "Just because you have not seen a thing doesn't mean it doesn't exist," she always said.

Years later she got a wonderful surprise. While in the country of Holland, Mrs. Bethune was given the bulbs of black tulips, the first black flower. And in Switzerland Mrs. Bethune was shown the black rose. This made her very happy. She ordered seventy-two black rose bushes. They were planted at Bethune-Cookman College. She also had black tulips planted at the entrance of her school.

CHAPTER 5

FROM COTTON FIELDS TO THE WHITE HOUSE

In 1932 Franklin D. Roosevelt was elected **president** of the United States. The president asked Mrs. Bethune to serve in the **National Youth Administration** (NYA). This organization helped people ages sixteen to twenty-four find part-time jobs. Mrs. Bethune was the first African-American woman to hold a job that high up in the government. It was an honor.

Mrs. Eleanor Roosevelt was the president's wife. She was a friend to Mrs. Bethune. At the time, some people didn't think a black person should be invited to the White House. But the Roosevelts did. Mrs. Bethune was always welcome at the White House and in the **Oval Office**, too.

As a teacher and a leader, Mrs. Bethune spent her life helping young people.

Once Mrs. Bethune went to see the president. "It is good to see you," he said. "I don't know why," Mrs. Bethune replied. "I'm always asking for something."

"Yes," said the president, "but you never ask for yourself."

It was true. Mrs. Bethune worked hard in the NYA. She tried to help young students find work so they could go to school. On April 25, 1945, Mrs. Bethune took part in the founding of the **United Nations**. Countries from all over the world agreed to work together for peace.

Mrs. Bethune lived the rest of her life at Bethune-Cookman College. There she died of a **heart attack** on May 18, 1955.

The school that Mary McLeod Bethune started with $1.50 is still in Daytona Beach. It helps prove that hard work can make dreams come true.

Words to Know

heart attack—An illness caused when the heart stops working properly. A person can die from a heart attack.

Moody Bible College—A college in Chicago started in 1886. It is now called the Moody Bible Institute.

National Youth Administration (NYA)—An organization that helps young people.

Oval Office—The American president's office. It is oval-shaped.

president—The leader of a country or group.

Scotia Seminary—An all-black school started in 1867 to teach former slaves and their children.

slave—A person who is owned by another. That person can be bought or sold.

United Nations—An organization of many countries who work together for peace.

White House—The house where the president of the United States lives.

LEARN MORE

Books

Evento, Susan. *Mary McLeod Bethune.* New York: Children's Press, 2004.

Jones, Amy Robin. *Mary McLeod Bethune.* Chanhassen, Minn.: Child's World, Inc., 2009.

McLoone, Margo. *Mary McLeod Bethune.* Mankato, Minn.: Capstone Press, 2006.

Web Sites

Mary McLeod Bethune Council House
<http://www.nps.gov/mamc/historyculture/people_marymcleodbethune.htm>

Bethune-Cookman College
<http://www.cookman.edu/about_bcu/history/our_founder.html>

National Women's Hall of Fame
<http://www.greatwomen.org/women-of-the-hall/search-the-hall/details/2/17-Bethune>

INDEX